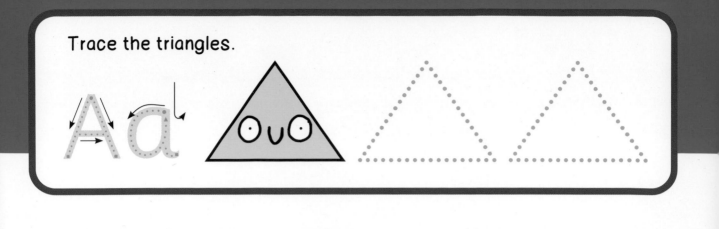

Trace the triangles.

Follow the trail to help
Anteater snack on ants.

Can you spot an ant
wearing a hat?

FINISH

START

Anteater

Ant

Now try tracing these:

A A A A A A

Trace the spirals.

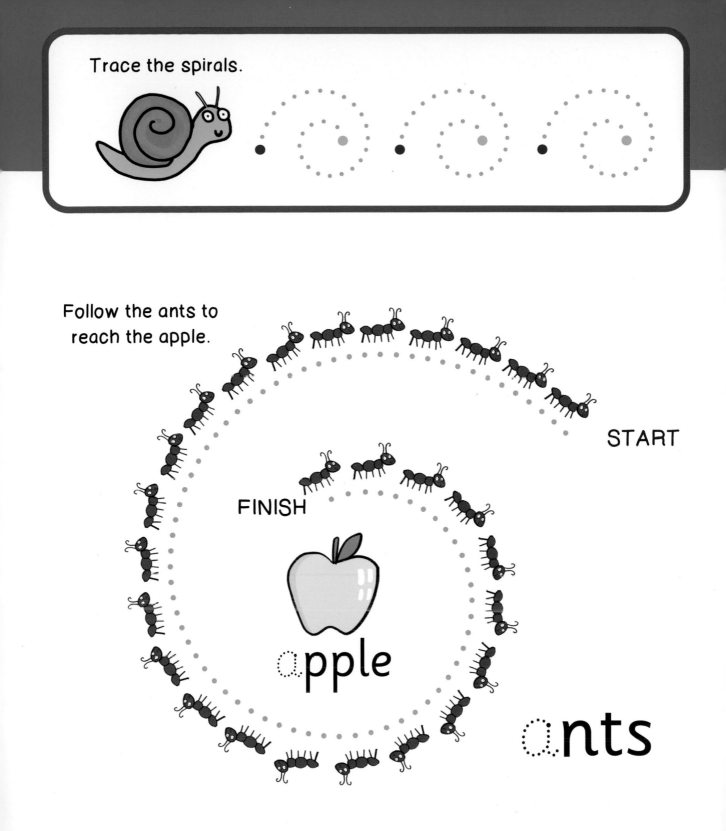

Follow the ants to
reach the apple.

START

FINISH

apple

ants

Now try tracing these:

a a a a a a

Trace the pattern.

Finish the beautiful butterfly.

Butterfly

Now try tracing these:

B B B B B B

Trace the pattern.

Trace the trails below.

balloon

bee

ball

Now try tracing these:

b b b b b b

Trace the pattern.

Trace the things below. Circle the
one that doesn't begin with C.

Cloud

What do you call
a sheep with no
legs?

A cloud!

Sheep

Crab

Now try tracing these:

Trace the pattern.

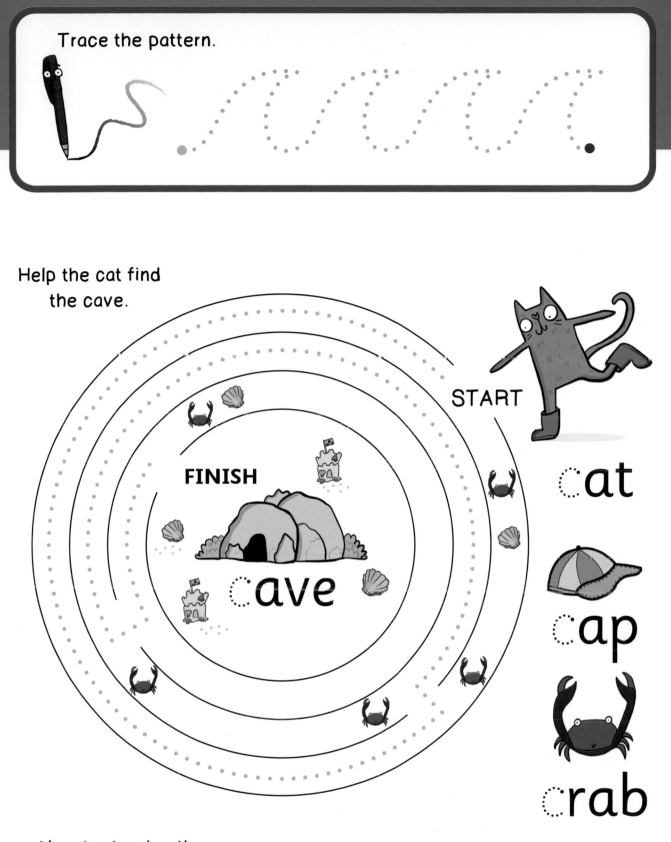

Help the cat find the cave.

START

FINISH

cave

cat

cap

crab

Now try tracing these:

c c c c c c c

Trace the pattern.

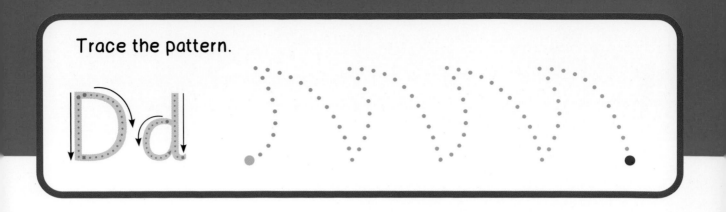

Circle the odd one out.

Dogs Dinosaur

Now try tracing these:

D D D D D D

Trace the pattern.

Trace the **d**'s in these words.

bed

teddy

dig

duck

d   d   d   d   d   d

Trace the pattern.

Finish the drawing of Ed Elephant. Trace the water to help him make a big splash.

Ed Elephant

Trace the pattern.

What color are the snails? Draw lines from the snails to match them to their color.

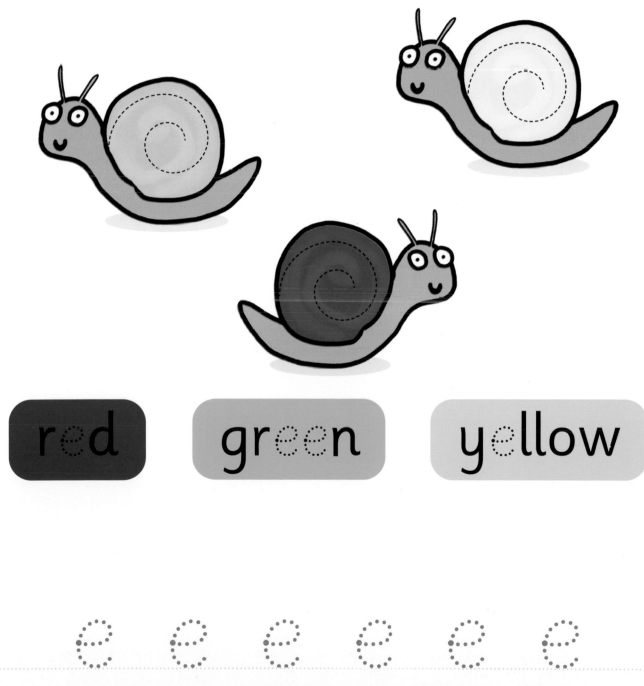

red   green   yellow

e   e   e   e   e   e

Trace the pattern.

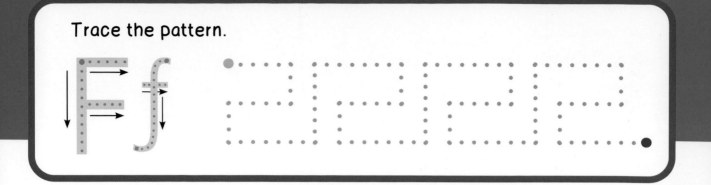

Help Fiona Frog visit the lily pads in alphabetical order.

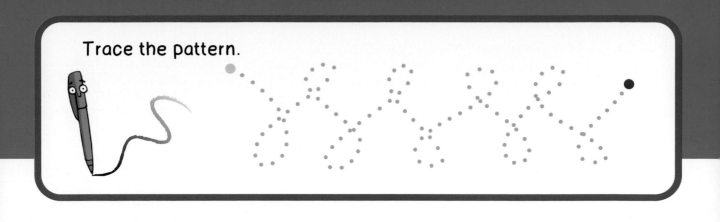

Trace the correct trail to help the fisherman catch the fish.

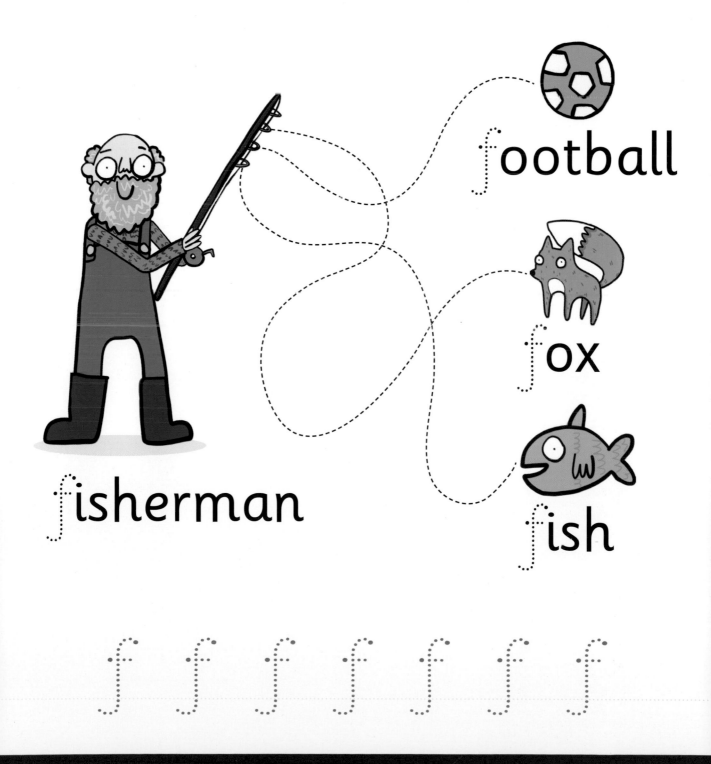

football

fox

fish

fisherman

f f f f f f

Trace the pattern.

G g

What color is Gertie Goat?
Circle your answer.

Gertie
Goat

BLUE   PINK   GRAY

G   G   G   G   G

Trace the pattern.

Trace the **g** in these words. Then trace the lines to show whether each word has a **g** at the beginning or at the end.

g at the beginning

g at the end

grapes

girl

frog

goat

dog

big

g   g   g   g   g

Trace the pattern.

Circle the light bulb that isn't working. Trace the ladder to help Harry fix it.

High

Harry

Fill in the **h**'s in this picture.

house

hill

horse

hedgehog

hay

h h h h h h

Trace the pattern.

I i | | | | | | | | | |

What color is Iggy Pig?
Circle your answer.

OINK!
I AM
IGGY!

RED   BLUE   PINK

I I I I I I I

Trace the lines to match the rhyming words.

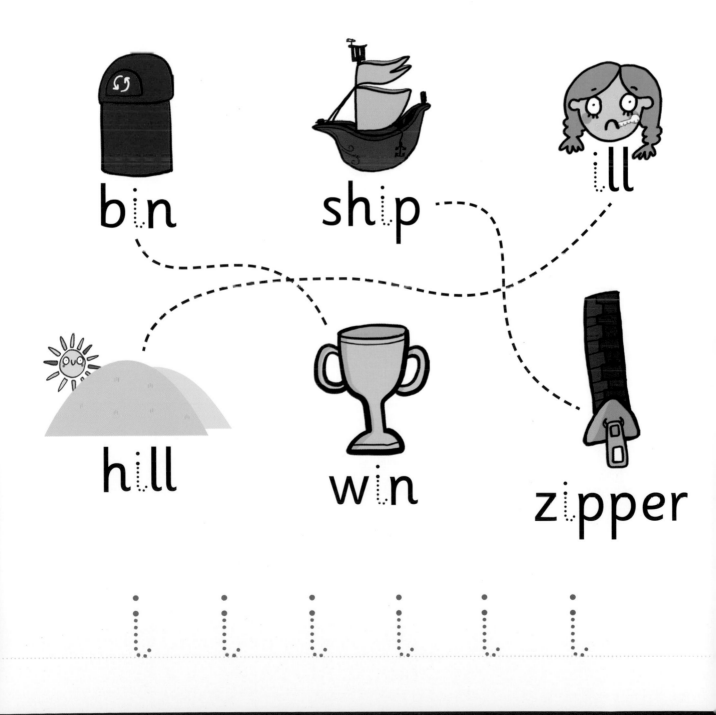

bin

ship

ill

hill

win

zipper

Connect the dots in alphabetical order from **A** to **J**.

Jumbo Jet

Trace the pattern.

Circle 4 differences between the jack-in-the-boxes.

jack-in-the-box

Trace the pattern.

Trace the patterns on
King Kevin's socks. Then draw
lines to match the pairs.

King Kevin

Trace the pattern.

Circle the things in the picture that start with k.

k k k k k k

Spot 4 differences between
the two pictures.

Leopard Lemur Lion

ladybug leaves

Trace the pattern.

Help Mr. Mole find his way back to his hole.

START

Mr. Mole

FINISH

Map

Mouse

Mop

Spot 3 things beginning with M in Mr. Mole's hole.

M M M M M M

Finish these monster portraits.

monsters

m m m m m m m

Trace the pattern.

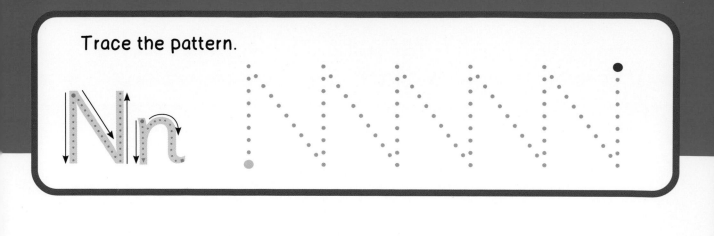

Trace the way through the maze
to help Nat reach Ned.

Ned

FINISH

Nat

START

N N N N N N

Trace the pattern.

Draw lines to show which teddies are new and which teddies are not new.

Trace the pattern.

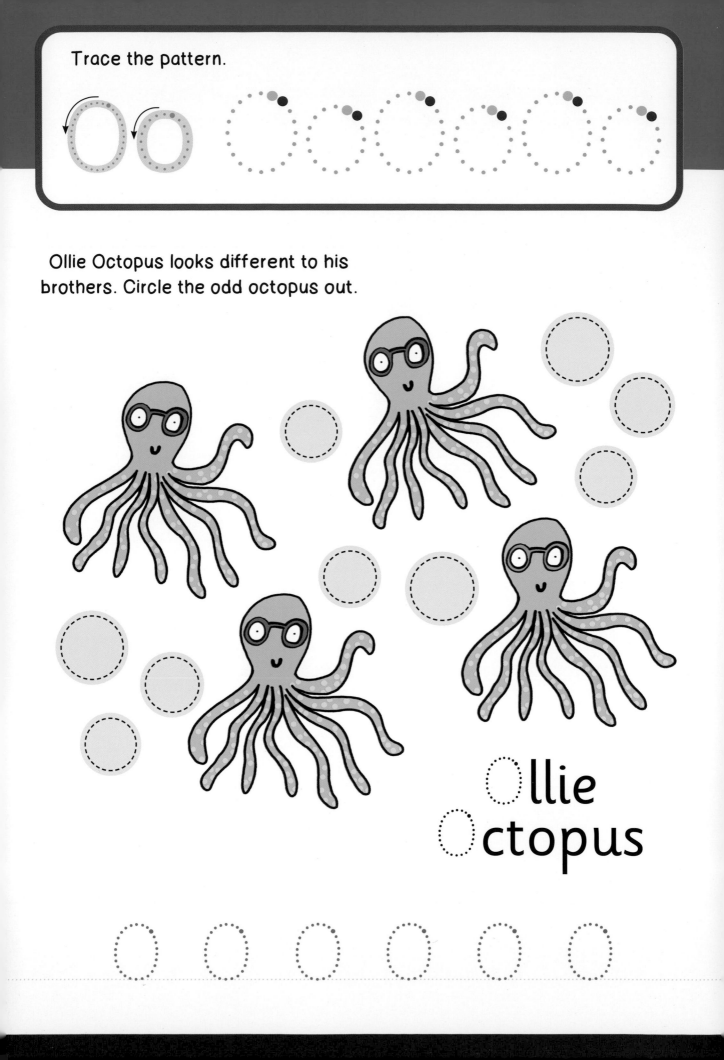

Ollie Octopus looks different to his brothers. Circle the odd octopus out.

Ollie
Octopus

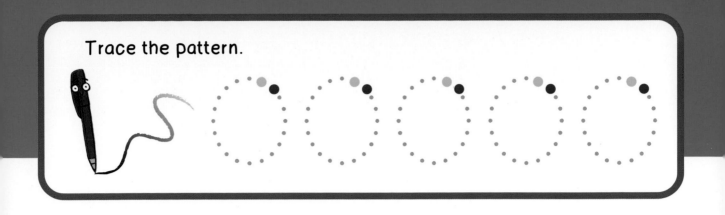

Circle all the things that are orange.

orange

Trace the pattern.

Which line leads to Pirate Pogo's favorite party food?

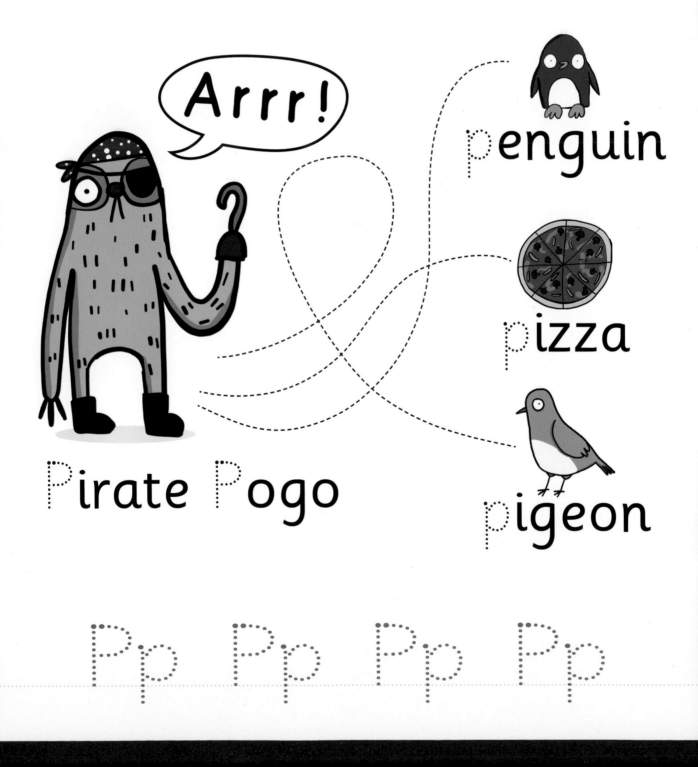

Arrr!

Pirate Pogo

penguin

pizza

pigeon

Pp   Pp   Pp   Pp

Trace the pattern.

Circle the thing below that is quick.

quick

Circle the thing below that is quiet.

quiet

Woof!

Quack!

Trace the pattern.

R r

Trace the tracks.
Which race car
wins the trophy?

red
race car

R r R r R r R r

Trace the pattern.

Trace the **u** in these words.

umbrella

bus

duck

Trace the pattern.

Follow the road to help the van reach the vet.

START

van

FINISH

vet

Trace the pattern.

Connect the dots in alphabetical order from **a** to **w**.

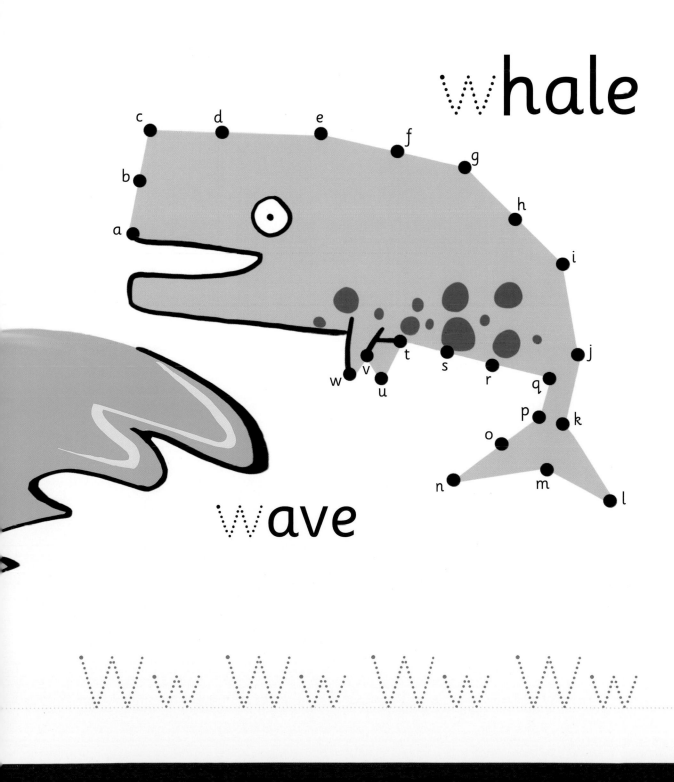

whale

wave

Trace the pattern.

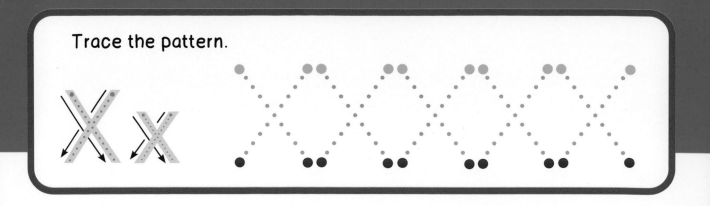

Circle the thing that starts with **x**.

box

x-ray

fox

Trace the pattern.

Circle the thing that starts with y.

lemon   lion   yo-yo

What color are all the things above?

YELLOW   RED   GREEN

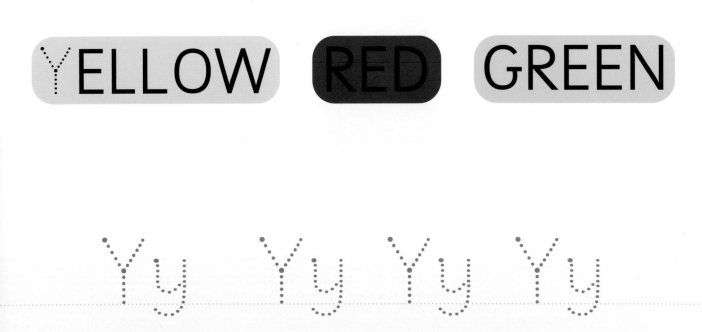

Yy Yy Yy Yy

Trace the pattern.

Trace the trails.

What noise does
a bee make?

bu**zz**

What noise does
a race car make?

zoom

Zz Zz Zz Zz

The alphabet

Now trace all the lowercase letters of the alphabet.

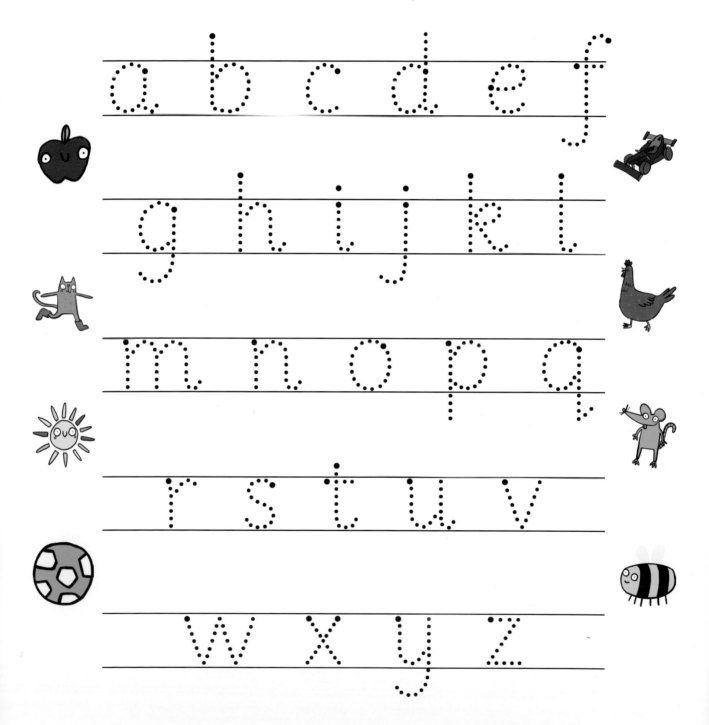

a b c d e f

g h i j k l

m n o p q

r s t u v

w x y z

CAPITAL LETTERS

Now trace all the uppercase letters of the alphabet.

A B C D E F

G H I J K L

M N O P Q

R S T U V W

X Y Z

All about you

Draw a picture of your face in the picture frame, then trace the words.

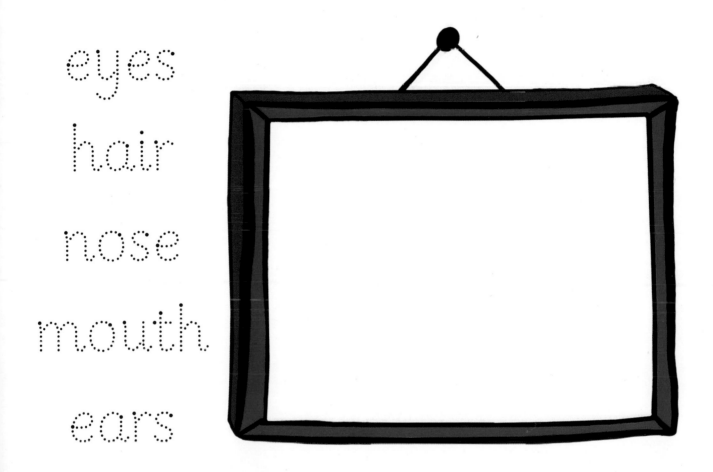

eyes

hair

nose

mouth

ears

Now write your name:

. . . .

Give your child a head start at school with this big book of games and activities, reviewed by educational experts. Then wipe the pages clean, and play all over again!

PUBLISHING

ISBN 978-1-83852-786-0

50899

9 781838 527860